This book belongs to:

_____

_____

Add your name here.
Make each letter
a different color
of the spectrum
(see page 36).

THIS IS NOT A SCIENCE BOOK

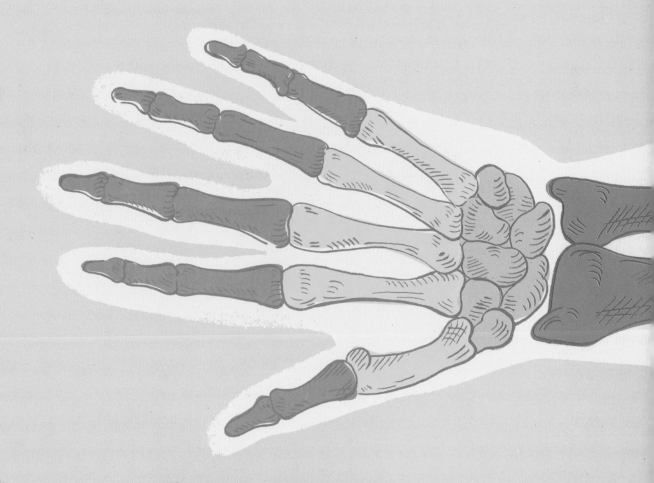

Kane Miller
A DIVISION OF EDC PUBLISHING

Clive Gifford

Illustrated by Charlotte Milner

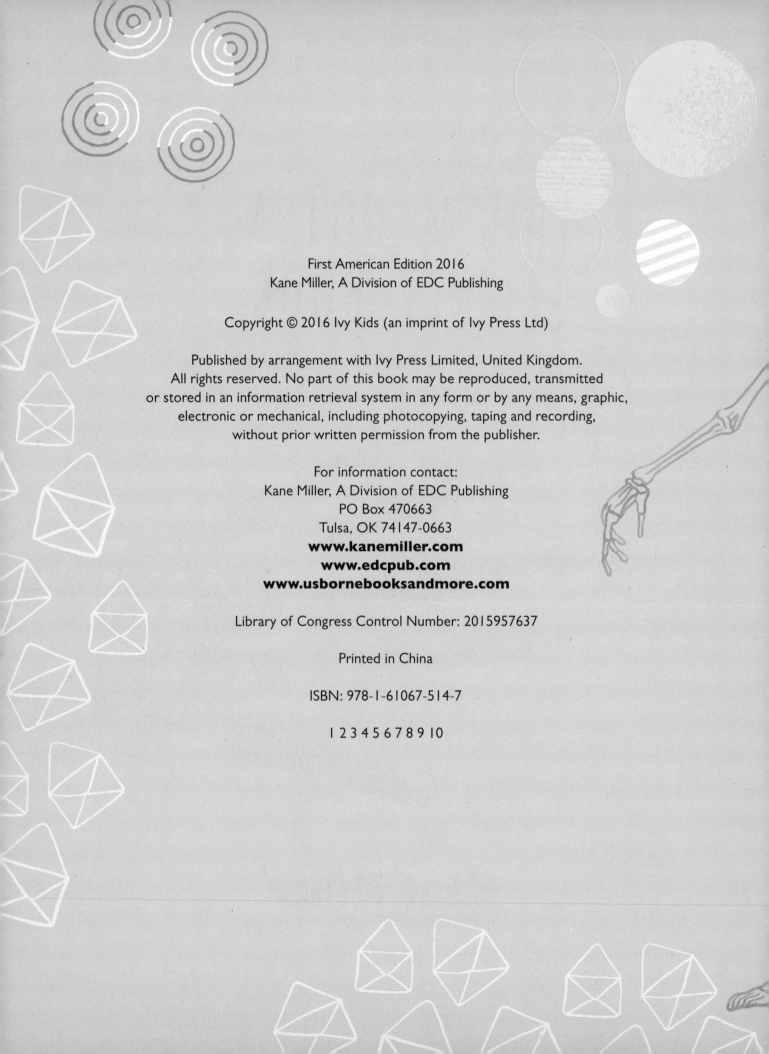

First American Edition 2016
Kane Miller, A Division of EDC Publishing

Copyright © 2016 Ivy Kids (an imprint of Ivy Press Ltd)

For information contact:
Kane Miller, A Division of EDC Publishing
PO Box 470663
Tulsa, OK 74147-0663
www.kanemiller.com
www.edcpub.com
www.usbornebooksandmore.com

Library of Congress Control Number: 2015957637

Printed in China

ISBN: 978-1-61067-514-7

1 2 3 4 5 6 7 8 9 10

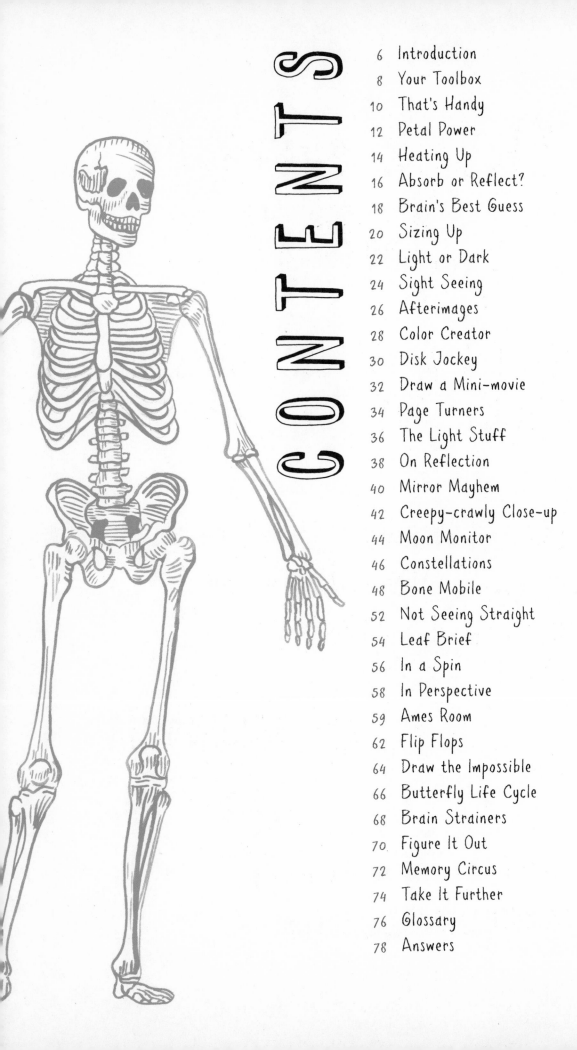

CONTENTS

Think science is stuffy?

WELL, RELAX, BECAUSE THIS IS NOT A SCIENCE BOOK... OR IS IT?

You see, there's so much more to science than lab coats, test tubes and textbooks.

SCIENCE IS **ALL AROUND US**,

and science can be FASCINATING and FUN!

Science is unbelievably important because it explains how the world around us works—from how we see and how light is made from lots of different colors, to how planes fly and how different creatures, including humans, live. Science has been used by clever people to provide us with many of the things we enjoy, from marvelous movies to terrific tricks and illusions.

This book is all about using fun activities to help make sense of science. It encourages you to explore the world around you through drawing, coloring and creating. Among other things, you'll learn how plants reproduce, discover the ways creatures change during their lives, and investigate scientific phenomena such as light and mirrors.

Packed with exciting projects, you'll observe the Moon, map out the bones in your body, test how heat can be reflected or absorbed, and challenge your brain with some awesome optical illusions and brain-bending puzzles.

SO, GRAB A PENCIL OR PEN, TURN THE PAGES
AND TRY OUT THIS CREATIVE COLLECTION OF
SCIENCE ACTIVITIES. THEY MAY HELP YOU
SEE SCIENCE IN A WHOLE NEW WAY!

YOUR TOOLBOX

YOU ONLY NEED A FEW THINGS TO COMPLETE THE SCIENCE ACTIVITIES IN THIS BOOK.

COLORING PENS AND CRAYONS: you'll need these for drawing, coloring, creating optical illusions and completing puzzles.

PENCIL AND ERASER: use a pencil for puzzles and challenges where you may need to erase your first attempt and try again.

CARDBOARD AND PAPER: you'll need cardboard and paper to make some of the projects.

TRACING PAPER: sometimes you'll be asked to trace a template in the book onto cardboard or paper. Learn how to do this on the opposite page.

SAFETY!
Some activities in this book use scissors or a sharp point, and may need an adult helper.

COMPASS: this tool is used for drawing perfect circles. It looks like an upside down V. On one leg of the V there's a pencil, and on the other leg there's a spike. You press the spike into your paper, so that you can swing the pencil around a central point.

RULER AND SCISSORS: a 12-inch ruler and a small pair of paper scissors is best.

ODDS AND ENDS: occasionally a project will need an extra item such as string, a paper clip, a blunt pencil stub or a mirror. You should be able to find these things around your home.

TEMPLATES

YOU CAN EITHER TRACE THE TEMPLATES OR, ALTERNATIVELY, THERE ARE TEMPLATES YOU CAN CUT OUT AT THE BACK OF THE BOOK. THESE CAN THEN BE STUCK ONTO CARDBOARD IF NECESSARY. IF YOU TRACE THEM, HERE'S HOW TO DO IT:

* Place the tracing paper over the template. Use a pencil to "trace" along the lines of the template, so that you end up with a copy of the template on your sheet of tracing paper.

* Turn over the tracing paper and place it facedown on a blank sheet of paper or cardboard. Hold it in place with some paper clips.

* Use a pencil to re-trace over all the lines again, pressing down firmly. The pencil marks on the tracing paper will be transferred to the sheet of paper or cardboard.

* You can now cut out your template.

THAT'S HANDY

DID YOU KNOW THAT YOUR BODY CONTAINS OVER 200 BONES AND JUST OVER HALF OF THESE ARE FOUND IN YOUR HANDS AND FEET?

1 Place your non-writing hand on the page.

2 Trace around it carefully, using a pen or pencil.

3 Using the diagram opposite, draw in your bones, starting with your fingers.

Why not trace around your foot, too? Using the Internet to help you, can you draw in all 26 of your foot bones?

Your four fingers have three **PHALANGES** each. Your thumb has just two.

The phalanges are jointed at your knuckles to longer bones called **METACARPALS**.

Now draw the two rows of bones that form the base of your hands. These bones are called **CARPALS**.

If you like, you can add the start of the two long bones that stretch from your wrist to your elbow. The narrower of the two bones is called the **ULNA**.

EACH OF YOUR HANDS CONTAINS 27 BONES. THESE ARE CONNECTED AT JOINTS TO GIVE YOU AN AMAZINGLY WIDE RANGE OF MOVEMENT. YOU CAN PULL, PICK, TWIST AND GRIP WITH YOUR HAND AND FINGERS.

PETAL POWER

Flowers contain the male and female sex organs of a plant. Seeds to grow new plants are produced when tiny grains of pollen from the male parts of a flower reach the female parts of the flower. Scientists call this process pollination.

COLOR IN THE FLOWER BELOW TO MATCH THE KEY.

The male flower parts are known as **STAMENS,** made up of an anther on top of a stem called a filament.

PETALS are brightly colored and scented to attract insects, birds and other animals.

The **STIGMA** is part of the female part of the flower. It is often sticky so that pollen can stick to it.

An **ANTHER** contains pollen grains.

POLLEN sticks to an animal's body and gets moved from one flower to another.

The **OVARY** contains ovules, which become seeds after they have been fertilized with pollen.

SEPALS protect the young flower bud until its petals have grown.

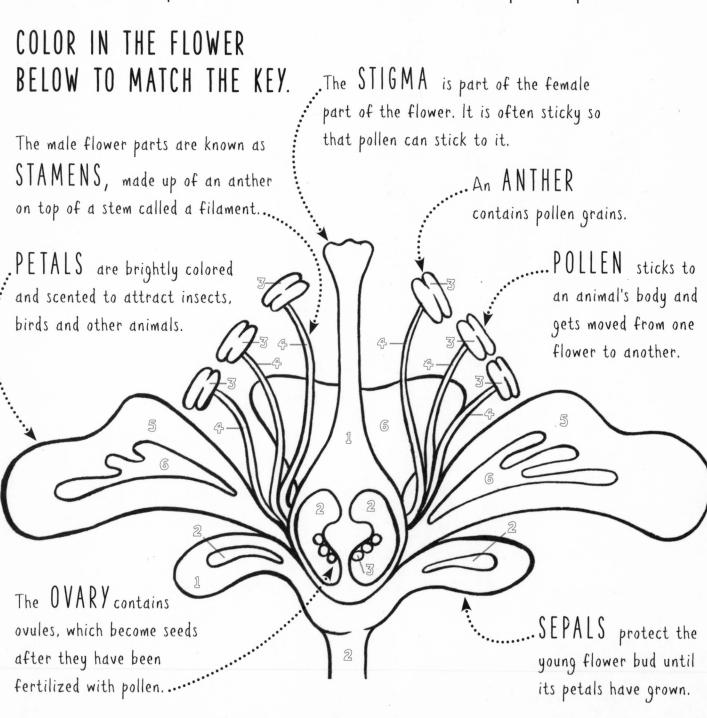

1 = 　　2 = 　　3 = 　　4 = 　　5 = 　　6 =

In Bloom

Flowers come in all shapes, colors and sizes. The petals of some flowers, such as daffodils, form a trumpet or bell shape. Other flowers, such as sunflowers, have large spread-out petals.

TAKE A LOOK AT SOME DIFFERENT TYPES OF FLOWERS GROWING NEAR YOU, AND DRAW THEM IN THE SPACES IN THE SCENE BELOW.

Add some bees buzzing around.

HEATING UP

HEAT IS A FORM OF ENERGY. HEATING SOMETHING UP GIVES IT MORE ENERGY.

Spinning Snake

HEAT MOVES INTO COOLER PLACES. THIS IS WHY A FURNACE WORKS TO HEAT YOUR HOME. AIR HEATED BY A FURNACE RISES, AND COOLER AIR MOVES IN TO TAKE ITS PLACE. THIS CREATES A FLOW OF MOVING AIR CALLED A CONVECTION CURRENT. YOU CAN SEE CONVECTION IN ACTION WITH THIS AMAZING SPINNING SNAKE!

1 Copy or trace the snake template onto thick white paper or thin cardboard, or use the template at the back of this book.

2 Cut carefully around the spiral and attach a piece of thread to the snake's head.

3 Hang your snake above a warm furnace and watch it spin.

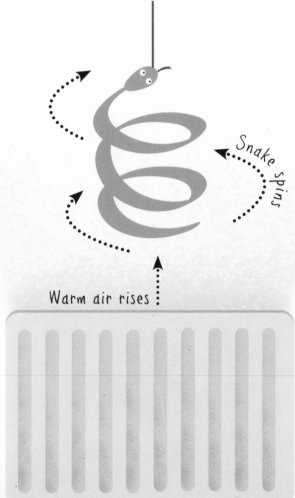

Snake spins

Warm air rises

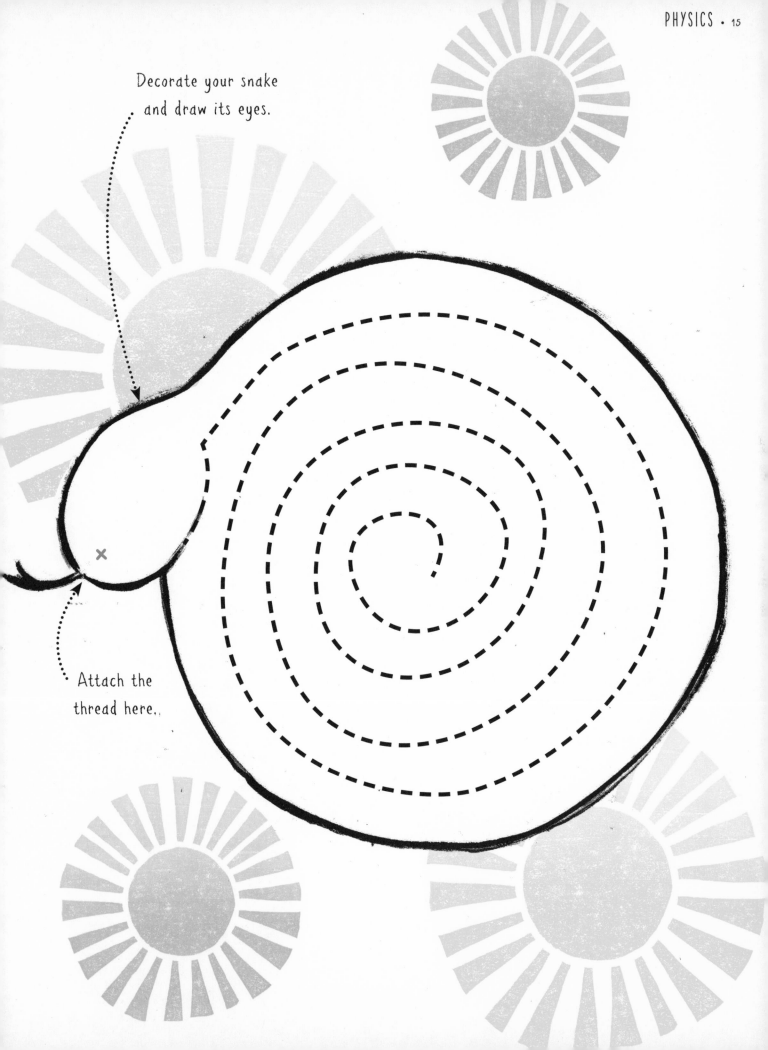

Decorate your snake and draw its eyes.

Attach the thread here.

ABSORB OR REFLECT?

OBJECTS CAN ABSORB HEAT AND BECOME HOTTER AS A RESULT. LEAVE THIS BOOK OPEN FOR AN HOUR ON A SUNNY DAY SO THAT DIRECT SUNLIGHT STRIKES THESE TWO PAGES. WHEN YOU RETURN, ONE PAGE SHOULD FEEL WARMER THAN THE OTHER.

The black page absorbs energy from the Sun and gets hotter. Lighter colors are better at reflecting the Sun's rays. This is the reason why many houses are painted white in hot countries.

Try using the power of the Sun to create some art. Cut out some paper shapes, and arrange them on this page to make a pattern. Then leave the book open in direct sunlight on a summer's day for as long as possible. The ultraviolet (UV) rays in the Sun's light will cause the chemical dyes found in the paper to fade, but the parts of the page covered by your shapes will stay the same!

BRAIN'S BEST GUESS

YOUR BRAIN IS CONSTANTLY BOMBARDED WITH INFORMATION FROM YOUR EYES. TO MANAGE THIS, IT OFTEN MAKES GUESSES ABOUT WHAT IT SEES, AND SOMETIMES IT IS WRONG. YOU CAN TRICK YOUR BRAIN INTO SEEING SHAPES THAT AREN'T ACTUALLY THERE. THESE ARE CALLED ILLUSORY CONTOURS.

1 Using a compass and a pencil, draw a circle at each of the points marked with a cross, matching their size with the circle already drawn.

2 Following the key below, turn each circle into a three-quarter circle by erasing part of the circle and then neatly drawing two straight lines that meet in the center.

3 Color all the three-quarter circles the same color. You should see a square lying on top of four circles—even though you didn't draw one!

WHY? YOUR BRAIN HAS CHOSEN A SQUARE ON TOP OF FOUR CIRCLES AS THE SIMPLEST EXPLANATION OF THE IMAGE SENT TO IT BY YOUR EYES.

Key:

Top right

Bottom left

Bottom right

HERE ARE SOME MORE EXAMPLES OF ILLUSORY CONTOUR
ILLUSIONS, CREATED USING DIFFERENT SHAPES AND
COLORS. CAN YOU DESIGN SOME OF YOUR OWN?

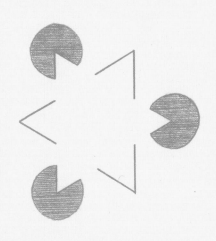

SIZING UP

YOUR BRAIN'S PRETTY GOOD AT ESTIMATING THE SIZE OF OBJECTS YOUR EYES SEE. SOMETIMES, THE ESTIMATE IS WRONG, AS THESE SIMPLE OPTICAL ILLUSIONS SHOW.

Circle Conundrum

Color all of the uncolored circles using the same color. Make sure the color you choose is different from the yellow central circles.

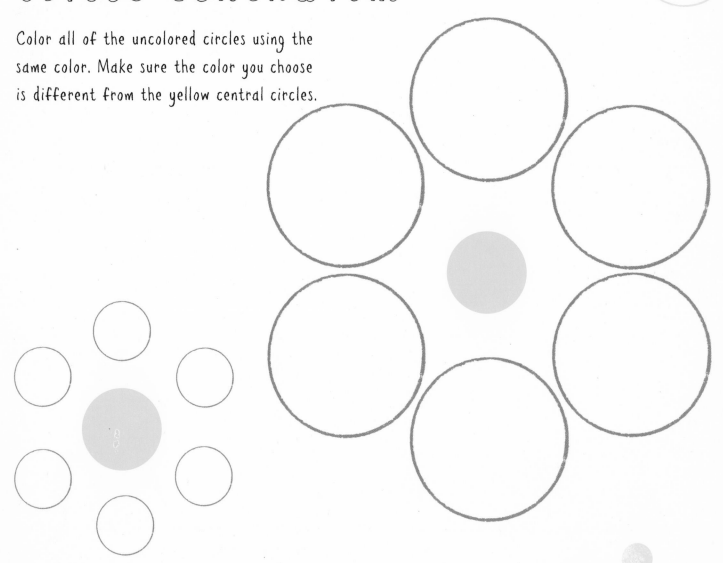

NOW ANSWER THIS QUESTION: WHICH YELLOW CIRCLE IS BIGGER?

THEY'RE ACTUALLY THE SAME SIZE. YOUR BRAIN CAN BE INFLUENCED BY THE SIZE OF NEIGHBORING OBJECTS. HERE THE SMALLER CIRCLES ON THE LEFT MAKE THE CIRCLE THEY SURROUND APPEAR BIGGER.

Which Line is Longer?

1 Add two slanting black lines like an arrow at each end of the top line.

Like this.

2 Now add an inward-pointing arrow to each end of the bottom line.

Like this.

THE BOTTOM LINE LOOKS LONGER, DOESN'T IT? BUT IF YOU MEASURE THE LINES WITH A RULER YOU'LL SEE THEY'RE THE EXACT SAME LENGTH.

A Lengthy Puzzle

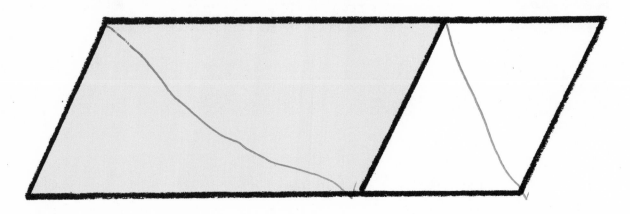

1 Add a straight blue line from the top left corner to the bottom right corner of the yellow shape.

2 Draw a straight red line from the bottom left corner to the top right corner of the uncolored shape.

WHICH LINE IS LONGER: BLUE OR RED? MOST PEOPLE WILL SAY THE BLUE, BUT BY NOW YOU WON'T BE SURPRISED TO DISCOVER THAT THEY ARE THE SAME LENGTH!

LIGHT OR DARK

ON THE PREVIOUS PAGE WE SAW HOW THE SIZE OF NEIGHBORING OBJECTS CAN TRICK YOUR BRAIN WHEN YOU'RE LOOKING AT AN IMAGE. ON THIS PAGE WE CAN SEE HOW NEIGHBORING COLORS CAN ALSO INFLUENCE WHAT YOUR BRAIN THINKS IT SEES.

Color Confusion

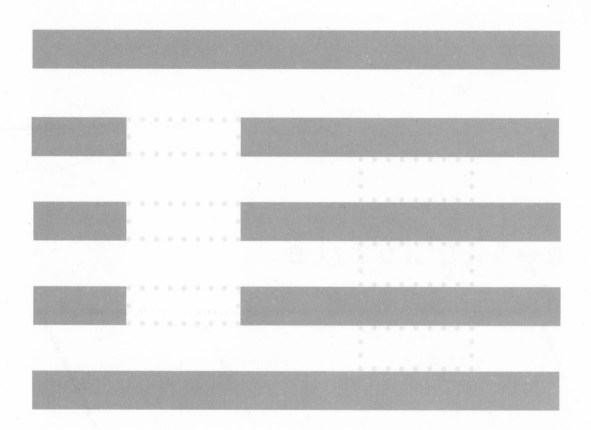

1 Using a bright-orange pen, solidly color in the six blank rectangular areas above.

2 Look at the completed image. The orange bars on the left look lighter even though they are the same color as those on the right ... as you know. After all, you did the coloring!

YOUR BRAIN'S VIEW OF THE ORANGE COLOR IS INFLUENCED BY THE BRIGHTNESS OF THE COLORS ABOVE AND BELOW IT.

Red Squares

NOW FIND A FINE-TIPPED RED PEN AND USE IT TO COLOR IN
ALL THE WHITE SQUARES IN THE TWO LARGE SQUARES BELOW.

YOU CAN SEE THE
COMPLETED ILLUSIONS
ON PAGE 78.

WHAT DO YOU SEE? THE RED SQUARES ARE PRECISELY THE SAME COLOR, BUT THOSE IN
THE BOTTOM SQUARE LOOK A LOT DARKER DUE TO THEIR SURROUNDINGS. **AMAZING!**

SIGHT SEEING

HOW DO YOU SEE?

Light enters your eye through a see-through protective covering called the cornea and passes through a small hole called the pupil. It travels through a disk-shaped lens which focuses the light on the retina at the back of your eye. There, special cells called rods and cones respond to the light and send signals to your brain along the optic nerve.

YOUR EYES' LENSES TURN THE IMAGE THEY SEE UPSIDE DOWN ON THE RETINA. YOUR BRAIN TURNS THE IMAGE RIGHT-SIDE UP.

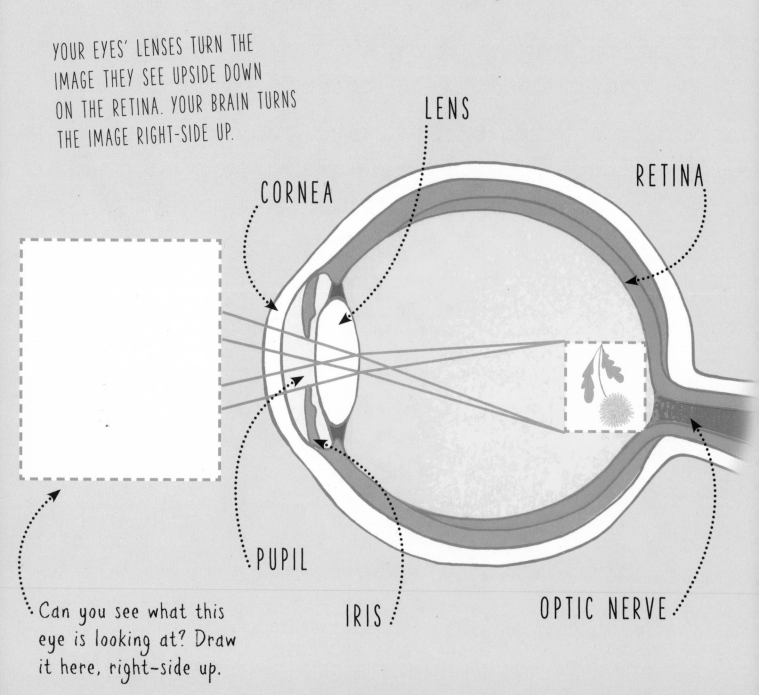

LENS

CORNEA

RETINA

PUPIL

IRIS

OPTIC NERVE

Can you see what this eye is looking at? Draw it here, right-side up.

Make a Rabbit Disappear

1 Using a pencil, draw a tiny rabbit, no more than ¾ inch in size, over the dot on the right and color it black-gray.

2 Hold the book at arm's length, close your left eye and focus on the large cross with your right eye.

3 Now, bring the book slowly up toward your right eye. The rabbit should disappear!

THIS HAPPENS WHEN THE IMAGE OF THE RABBIT REACHES YOUR EYE'S "BLIND SPOT" WHERE THE OPTIC NERVE JOINS THE BACK OF THE EYE. THIS SPOT DOESN'T HAVE ANY ROD AND CONE CELLS SO CAN'T SEE ANYTHING AT ALL.

Pupil Power

When it's dark or dim, the hole in your eye called the PUPIL gets bigger to let more light into your eye. The size of your pupil is controlled by a muscle called the IRIS—the colored part of the eye around the pupil.

AFTERIMAGES

Afterimages are pictures you can still see after you've stopped looking at them. Here you can create some afterimage illusions, which also make your eyes see colors that aren't even there. Crazy!

Apple of Your Eye

1 Color this apple using a bright light-blue pen, with bright pink for the leaf.

2 Stare at it for 45 seconds. Try to concentrate and do not let your eyes wander at all.

3 Turn away and look at a blank piece of white paper. WHAT DO YOU SEE?

A RED APPLE WITH A GREEN LEAF!

HOW COME?

SPECIAL CELLS (CALLED RODS AND CONES) AT THE BACK OF YOUR EYES HANDLE THE DIFFERENT COLORS OF LIGHT THAT REACH THEM. WHEN THEY GET TIRED OF STARING AT THE SAME COLOR FOR A LONG PERIOD OF TIME, OTHER CELLS NEAR THEM SEND SIGNALS TO THE BRAIN THAT FEATURE AN ALTERNATIVE COLOR (SEE OPPOSITE).

Changing Colors

Using pens, color in this Union Jack flag
(the flag of the United Kingdom).

Color the eight triangle
shapes bright yellow.

Color the remaining
white spaces light blue.

Stare at your completed image for 45 seconds,
then look at a blank piece of white paper.

YOU SHOULD SEE THE UNION JACK NOW IN ITS
CORRECT COLORS OF RED, WHITE AND BLUE.

WHY DID THE TRIANGLES YOU COLORED YELLOW APPEAR BLUE,
AND THE AREAS YOU COLORED LIGHT BLUE APPEAR RED?

Scientists call these pairs of colors "complementary colors," and
they appear opposite each other on a color wheel. In an
afterimage, you will see the complementary color of the
color you were first staring at.

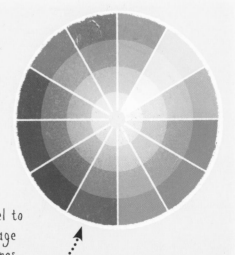

You can use a color wheel to
draw your own afterimage
flags or different pictures.

COLOR CREATOR

TURN BLACK AND WHITE INTO COLOR WITH THESE PUZZLING DISKS. BENHAM'S DISKS ARE NAMED AFTER AN ENGLISH TOYMAKER CALLED CHARLES BENHAM, WHO SOLD A SPINNING TOP PAINTED WITH DESIGNS LIKE THESE MORE THAN 100 YEARS AGO.

1 Trace the templates and their circular patterns onto white cardboard or use the templates at the back of this book. If you are copying the patterns, you can draw the curves freehand or use a compass.

2 Cut each of the circles out. With an adult's help, poke a small hole through the middle of each circle.

3 Ease a short, blunt pencil stub through the hole to create a simple spinning top.

4 Spin your top and watch closely. Most people will see pale colors such as blues, browns and yellows appear on the disk as it turns.

Try out different disks to find out if you see different colors.

SCIENTISTS MAY KNOW MANY THINGS, BUT THEY DON'T KNOW FOR CERTAIN WHY THIS EFFECT OCCURS! SOME THINK IT MIGHT BE DUE TO THE THREE DIFFERENT TYPES OF CONE CELLS IN YOUR EYES THAT DETECT COLORS. THESE WORK AT SLIGHTLY DIFFERENT SPEEDS, WHICH MIGHT EXPLAIN WHY TRACES OF COLOR ARE SEEN AS THE DISKS SPIN.

DISK JOCKEY

A THAUMATROPE WAS A SIMPLE, POPULAR TOY IN VICTORIAN TIMES. ITS NAME MEANS "WONDER TURNER" IN ANCIENT GREEK. IF YOU FLIP IT FAST ENOUGH, THE TWO IMAGES ON THE BACK AND FRONT OF THE DISK COMBINE TO MAKE A SINGLE IMAGE. **MAGIC!**

1 Trace the front and back of the disk template on the opposite page onto either side of a piece of thick white cardboard, or use the templates at the back of this book, and color in. Remember that the image on the back should be upside down.

2 With an adult's help, poke a small hole through each of the two yellow dots and thread a piece of elastic or a rubber band through each hole. You can use string instead if you prefer.

3 Twirl the elastic to spin the disk around and you'll see the two images merge into one!

You can photocopy the images, cut them out and glue them onto cardboard if you prefer.

HOW DOES IT WORK?

THE IMAGES THAT REACH THE BACK OF YOUR EYE LINGER FOR A FRACTION OF A SECOND. SCIENTISTS CALL THIS "PERSISTANCE OF VISION." WHEN THE THAUMATROPE IS SPUN QUICKLY, YOUR EYES FOCUS ON THE TWO DIFFERENT IMAGES JUST LONG ENOUGH TO MERGE THEM TOGETHER.

NOW TRY DESIGNING YOUR OWN THAUMATROPE!

You could put a fish in a bowl or a spider in a web, or perhaps add glasses or a moustache to a face— or try out your own ideas. You can use letters as well as pictures; try alternating the letters of your name so that the thaumatrope spells out your name when it is spun!

FRONT

BACK

DRAW A MINI-MOVIE

ON THE LAST PAGE WE SAW HOW PERSISTENCE OF VISION ALLOWS YOUR BRAIN TO MERGE TWO SEPARATE IMAGES INTO ONE. MOVIES WORK THE SAME WAY. A MOVIE IS A SERIES OF PICTURES SHOWN ONE AFTER THE OTHER WITH SMALL CHANGES BETWEEN EACH PICTURE. IF SHOWN QUICKLY ENOUGH, YOUR EYES AND BRAIN SEE THIS SERIES OF PICTURES AS A SINGLE MOVING IMAGE.

You can make a simple **flip book** of images that you flick through to create your own mini-movie.

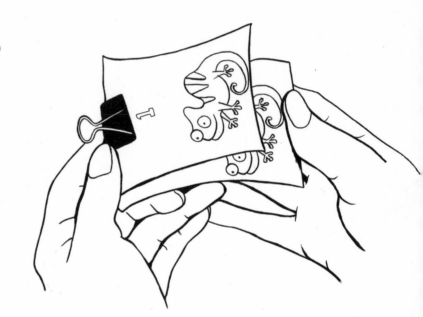

1 Trace the images on the right-hand page onto white paper or use the templates at the back of this book. Cut each image out.

2 Stack the images on top of each other, with number 20 on the bottom and number 1 on top. Make sure the bottom edges line up, and then clip them together at the top with a bulldog or binder clip.

HOLDING THE TOP OF THE BOOK WITH ONE HAND, FLIP THROUGH THE PAGES WITH YOUR THUMB. YOUR MOVIE SHOULD COME TO LIFE!

Now try creating your own bigger flip book! Cut up at least 20–30 pieces of paper into 4-inch x 4-inch squares, then stack and clip them together. Your movie should start with a drawing on the top page. Make small changes to your scene with each new drawing. Try out something simple at first, such as a stick figure playing.

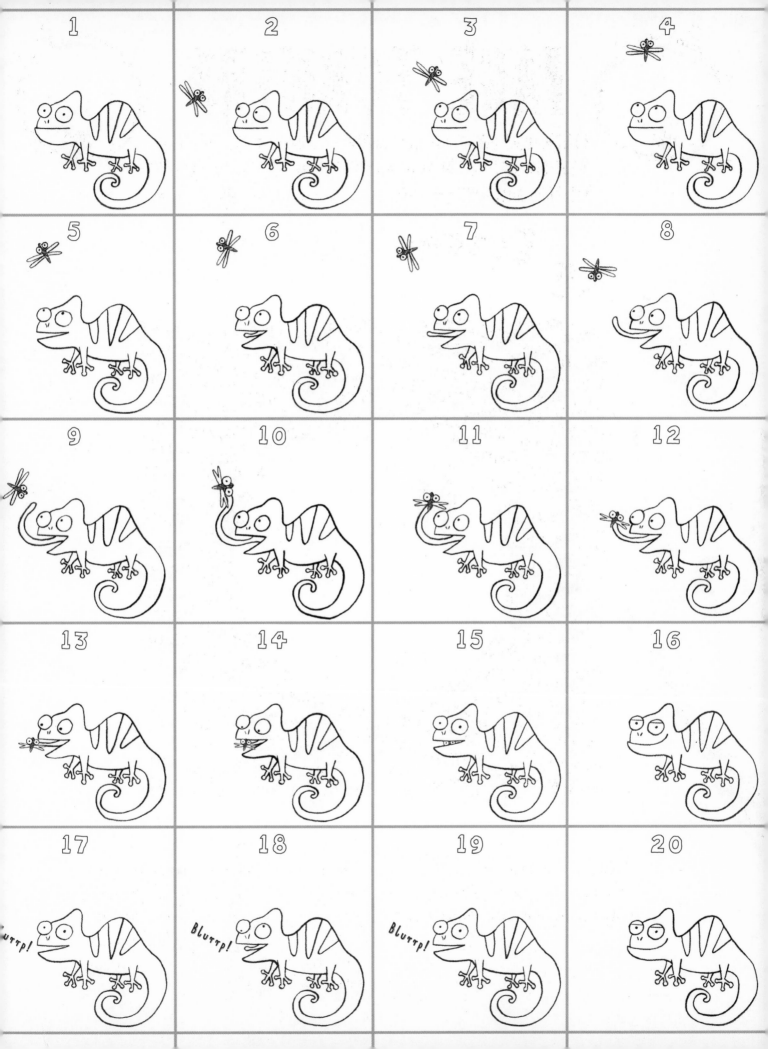

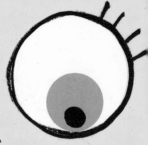

PAGE TURNERS

MOTION ILLUSIONS ACTUALLY APPEAR TO MOVE ON A STILL PAGE!
SCIENTISTS BELIEVE THESE WORK BECAUSE OF THE WAY YOUR EYES
FLIT BACK AND FORTH AS THEY SCAN THE SCENE AHEAD OF THEM.

Shifting Circle

YOU CAN SEE THE COMPLETED
ILLUSION ON PAGE 78.

1 Take a fine black pen or sharp dark pencil, and color in every gray rectangle in the center circle.

2 From above, look directly down and move your eyes left and right a little as you stare at the image. You should see the circle hover slightly above the background, while the background slips a little from side to side. WOW!

Spinning Rings

Continue this pattern, on both the outside and inside rings.

1 Using a fine black pen or sharp dark pencil, color in every other crescent (the ones shaded gray) on both rings.

2 When you have finished, stare at the image and let your eyes move around a little. Most people find that the two rings appear to move, as if turning around each other.

YOU CAN SEE THE COMPLETED ILLUSION ON PAGE 79.

THE LIGHT STUFF

Light is a form of energy and is made up of different colors, called the color spectrum. It travels in straight lines and fast—186,000 MILES PER SECOND!

When light hits an object, some of these colors are absorbed. Other colors reflect or bounce off, and these are the colors that give the object the color your eyes see!

All of these colors are absorbed by the lemon ...

... but yellow light bounces off, making the lemon appear yellow to us.

White light from the Sun is a mixture of the different colors of the spectrum. When this light passes through drops of water in the air, it bends and its colors separate, creating a RAINBOW!

Color these bands in order: red, orange, yellow, green, blue, indigo (dark blue) and violet (purple).

Make a Color Spinner

WE'VE SEEN HOW WHITE LIGHT CAN BE SPLIT UP INTO ITS INDIVIDUAL COLORS. WITH THIS CLEVER SPINNER YOU CAN RECOMBINE THE COLORS TO MAKE WHITE AGAIN!

1 Trace this circle onto thin white cardboard and then color it in with the different colors of the spectrum. Or, you can cut out the template at the back of this book.

2 Cut your circle out. With an adult's help, either poke a small hole through the middle and push a small pencil stub through the hole, or make two small holes in the center and thread a large rubber band, a piece of elastic or string through the holes.

3 Spin your disk nice and fast. The colors should all merge and disappear, and the disk will appear white. Magic!

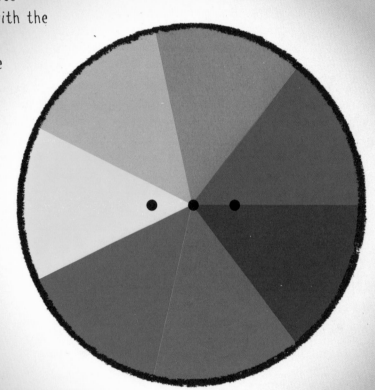

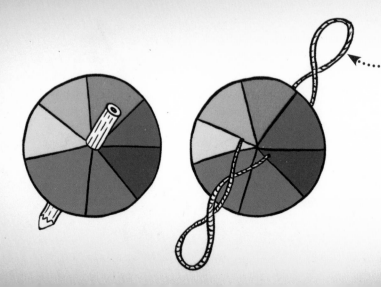

Place your index finger through the loop at each end of the rubber band, and flip the disk over in a circular motion until the band is twisted. Pull the rubber band tight to make the disk spin!

ON REFLECTION

ON REFLECTION

MIRRORS ARE SHINY SURFACES THAT CAUSE ALMOST ALL THE LIGHT THAT HITS THEM TO REFLECT (BOUNCE OFF). MANY THINGS CAN ACT LIKE A MIRROR, INCLUDING POLISHED METAL OR THE BACK OF A LARGE SPOON!

Funny Face

1 Get as large and curved a spoon or ladle as you can find and bring the outside of it up close to your face.

2 Can you draw how your face looks in this frame?

THE SPOON REFLECTS BACK YOUR IMAGE, BUT BECAUSE IT IS CURVED IT DISTORTS YOUR FEATURES. MOST MIRRORS ARE FLAT TO BOUNCE OFF LIGHT WITH AS LITTLE DISTORTION AS POSSIBLE.

Mirror Image

WHEN YOU STAND DIRECTLY IN FRONT OF A MIRROR, YOUR EYES SEE LIGHT BOUNCED STRAIGHT BACK. WHAT YOU SEE IS A MIRROR IMAGE— ALMOST IDENTICAL TO WHAT YOU LOOK LIKE IN REAL LIFE, BUT WITH LEFT AND RIGHT REVERSED.

YOU CAN USE A MIRROR IMAGE TO COMPLETE HALF A DRAWING.

1 Place a mirror along the dotted line, facing the drawing. If you're left-handed it might be easier to complete the drawing upside down.

2 Look down the mirror and copy the image you see on the paper to the right of the mirror.

MIRROR MAYHEM

CHALLENGE YOUR BRAIN AND HAND-EYE COORDINATION BY TRACING
A STAR SHAPE USING ONLY A MIRROR IMAGE AS YOUR GUIDE.

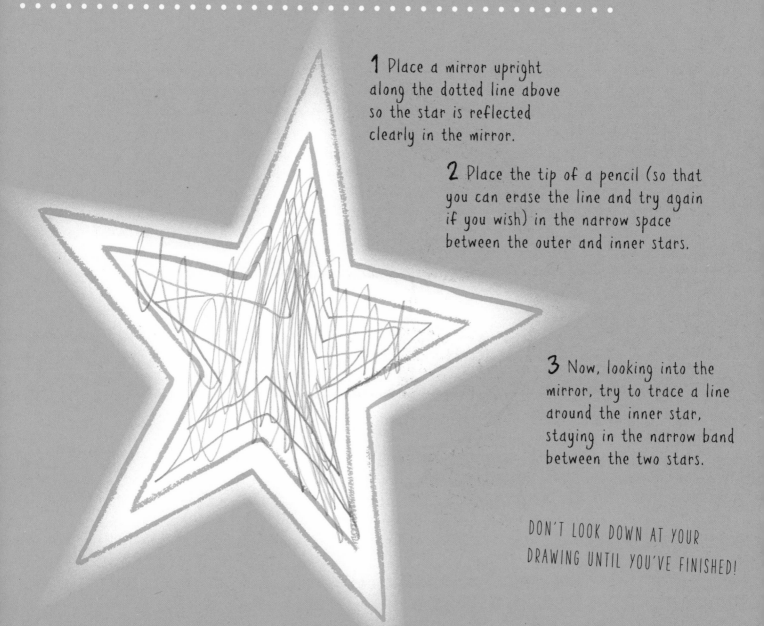

1 Place a mirror upright along the dotted line above so the star is reflected clearly in the mirror.

2 Place the tip of a pencil (so that you can erase the line and try again if you wish) in the narrow space between the outer and inner stars.

3 Now, looking into the mirror, try to trace a line around the inner star, staying in the narrow band between the two stars.

DON'T LOOK DOWN AT YOUR DRAWING UNTIL YOU'VE FINISHED!

HOW DID YOU DO?

Most people find they make mistakes, especially when changing direction as they draw. This is because your brain is receiving different information than usual. The mirror flips or reverses the image so that the top of the star becomes the bottom and the left side becomes the right. This makes it harder to copy at first, but your brain learns quickly and it gets easier.

Bouncing Around

MIRRORS AT AN ANGLE CAN BOUNCE LIGHT
IN DIFFERENT DIRECTIONS. PERISCOPES,
TELESCOPES AND SOME CAMERAS USE
MIRRORS TO BOUNCE LIGHT IN THIS WAY.

A mirror at a 45-degree
angle bounces light
off at a right angle
(90 degrees).

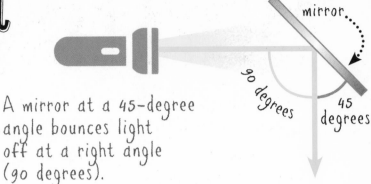

Mirrors are being used to bounce light around this maze below. Can you plot
the path of each of the three beams of light as they bounce off the mirrors
and travel through the maze, so that each reaches its matching target?

Start off by completing the blue
beam's path through the maze.

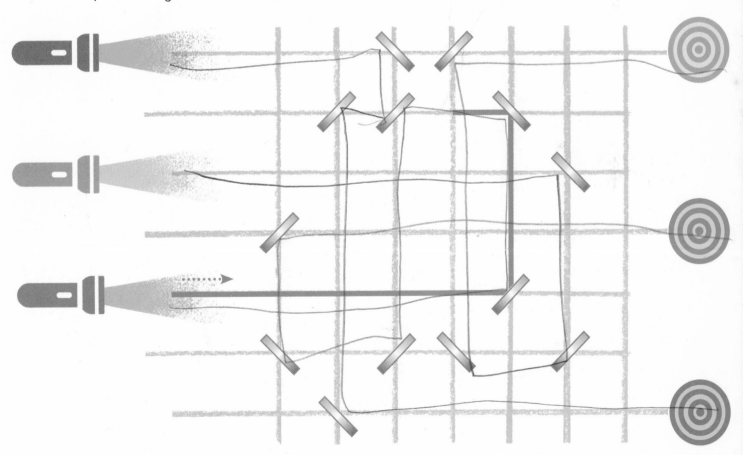

REMEMBER! Each time a light beam hits a mirror,
it will bounce off at a right angle.

YOU CAN FIND THE
ANSWER ON PAGE 79.

CREEPY-CRAWLY CLOSE-UP

There are more types of insects than any other creature on Earth. Millions of kinds exist, including cockroaches, beetles, crickets, flies, ants and bees. They range in size from the tiny fairyfly, which is just .02 inch long, to giant dragonflies with wingspans of more than 7 inches.

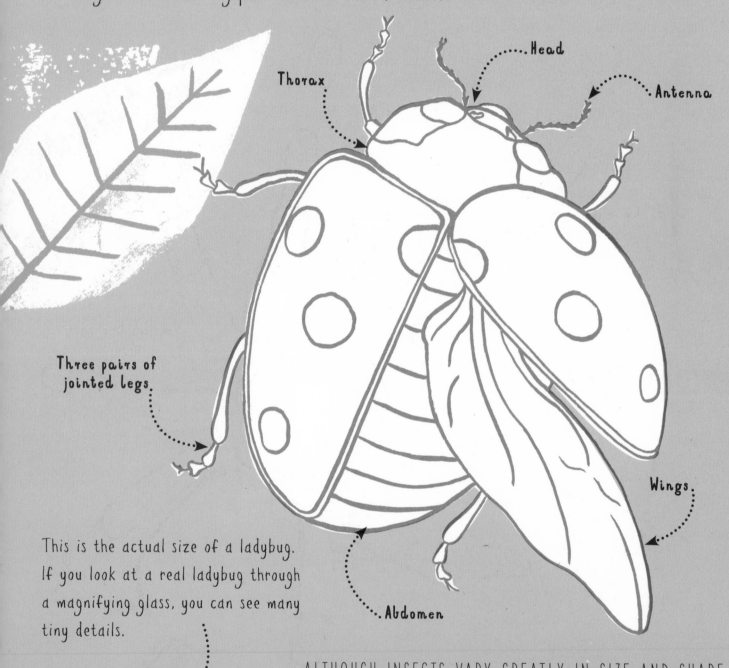

Thorax

Head

Antenna

Three pairs of jointed legs

Wings

This is the actual size of a ladybug. If you look at a real ladybug through a magnifying glass, you can see many tiny details.

Abdomen

ALTHOUGH INSECTS VARY GREATLY IN SIZE AND SHAPE, THEY SHARE A NUMBER OF PARTS THAT YOU CAN SEE IN THE IMAGE. COLOR THIS LADYBUG'S SPOTTED WINGS AND BLACK BODY, HEAD AND LEGS.

Spiders

Spiders are not insects! They are arachnids. Unlike insects, they don't have wings, and they have eight instead of six legs. Many spiders have eight eyes! The rear of their abdomen contains special parts that help the spider spin silk thread. This Mexican redknee tarantula spider can grow to 6 inches long. It feeds mostly on insects but also on small birds and lizards.

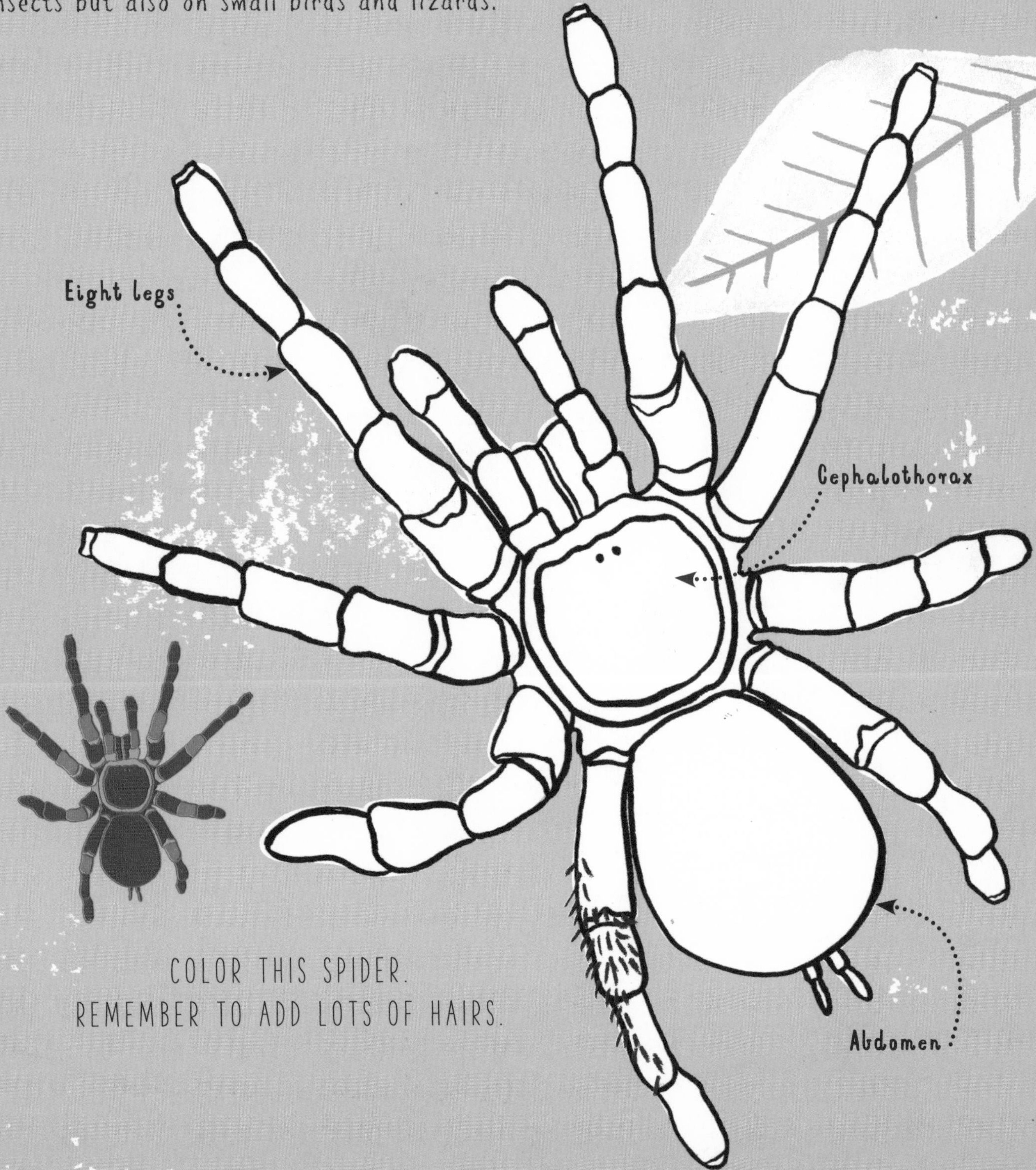

Eight legs

Cephalothorax

COLOR THIS SPIDER.
REMEMBER TO ADD LOTS OF HAIRS.

Abdomen

MOON MONITOR

The Moon travels on a path around Earth called an orbit. Just like Earth, half of the Moon is lit by the Sun while the other half is in darkness.

AS THE MOON TRAVELS AROUND EARTH, THE AMOUNT OF THE MOON WE CAN SEE ON EARTH CHANGES. THESE ARE CALLED PHASES AND EACH HAS A NAME.

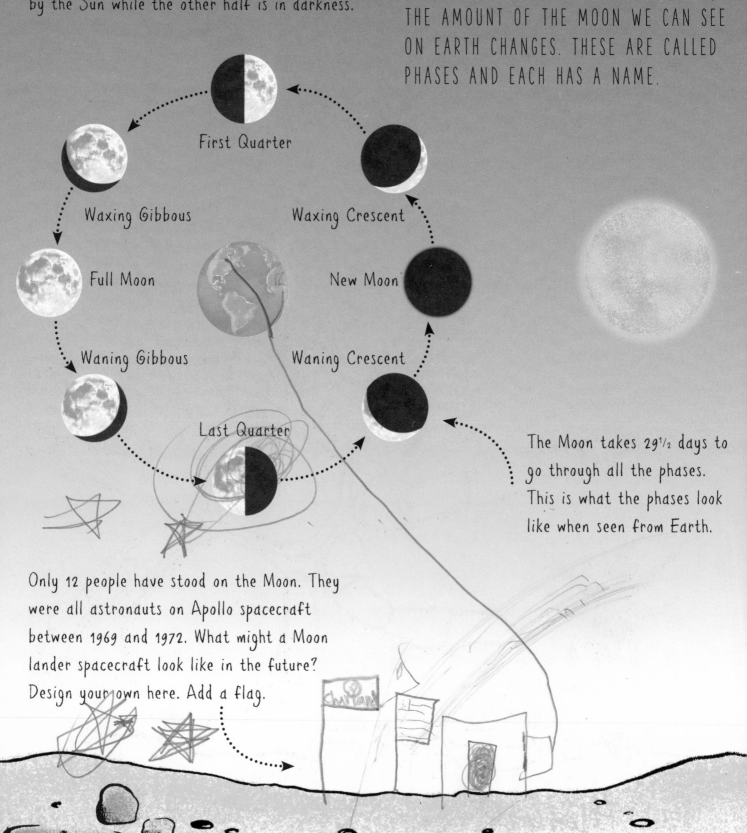

First Quarter

Waxing Gibbous

Waxing Crescent

Full Moon

New Moon

Waning Gibbous

Waning Crescent

Last Quarter

The Moon takes 29½ days to go through all the phases. This is what the phases look like when seen from Earth.

Only 12 people have stood on the Moon. They were all astronauts on Apollo spacecraft between 1969 and 1972. What might a Moon lander spacecraft look like in the future? Design your own here. Add a flag.

Chart the Moon's Phases

FOR ONE MONTH, EVERY TWO OR THREE DAYS TAKE A
LOOK AT THE MOON AND RECORD WHAT YOU SEE BELOW.

Using a black pen, block
out the part of the
Moon you cannot see.

Add the date here.

The Moon's gravity is about one-sixth
of that on Earth. This means that if
you could jump 3 feet high on Earth,
you'd be able to jump 18 feet high
on the Moon!

CONSTELLATIONS

On a clear night, away from a city's lights, you can see 2,000 stars or more from Earth. Millions more exist though. A constellation is a group of stars that make an imaginary shape in the night sky. They are often named after animals, objects or characters from myths and legends.

CONNECT THE STARS BELOW TO FORM FAMOUS CONSTELLATION PATTERNS.

Orion

This constellation was named after a hunter called Orion in Greek myths because people thought that it looked like a man raising a sword and holding a shield.

7
6
5 & 12
4
8 11
1
3
2
9
10

Stars are giant balls of super-hot gas, which give off large amounts of heat and light. Their light travels across the Universe at 186,000 miles every second.

Our closest star is the Sun. It's quite small compared to some other stars. A star called Betelgeuse in the Orion constellation is thought to be more than 700 times bigger in size!

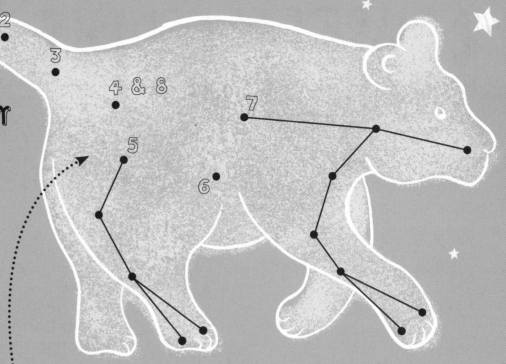

Ursa Major

Ursa Major is also known as the Great Bear. It contains a group of stars that form their own mini-pattern called the Big Dipper.

Complete the Ursa Major constellation by connecting the stars that make the Big Dipper.

Create Your Own Constellation

Make your own constellation by connecting some of the stars below. What shape does your constellation make? Name it!

One of our closest star neighbors is Alpha Centauri. It would take a spacecraft traveling at 17,400 mph about 165,000 years to reach it.

BONE MOBILE

Let's make a movable model mobile of your body's SKELETON—the bony frame inside you.

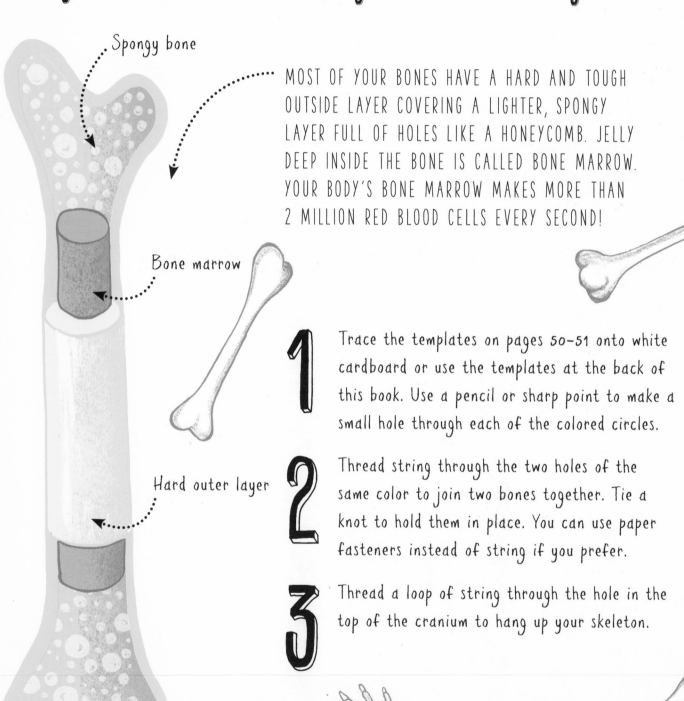

Spongy bone

MOST OF YOUR BONES HAVE A HARD AND TOUGH OUTSIDE LAYER COVERING A LIGHTER, SPONGY LAYER FULL OF HOLES LIKE A HONEYCOMB. JELLY DEEP INSIDE THE BONE IS CALLED BONE MARROW. YOUR BODY'S BONE MARROW MAKES MORE THAN 2 MILLION RED BLOOD CELLS EVERY SECOND!

Bone marrow

Hard outer layer

1 Trace the templates on pages 50-51 onto white cardboard or use the templates at the back of this book. Use a pencil or sharp point to make a small hole through each of the colored circles.

2 Thread string through the two holes of the same color to join two bones together. Tie a knot to hold them in place. You can use paper fasteners instead of string if you prefer.

3 Thread a loop of string through the hole in the top of the cranium to hang up your skeleton.

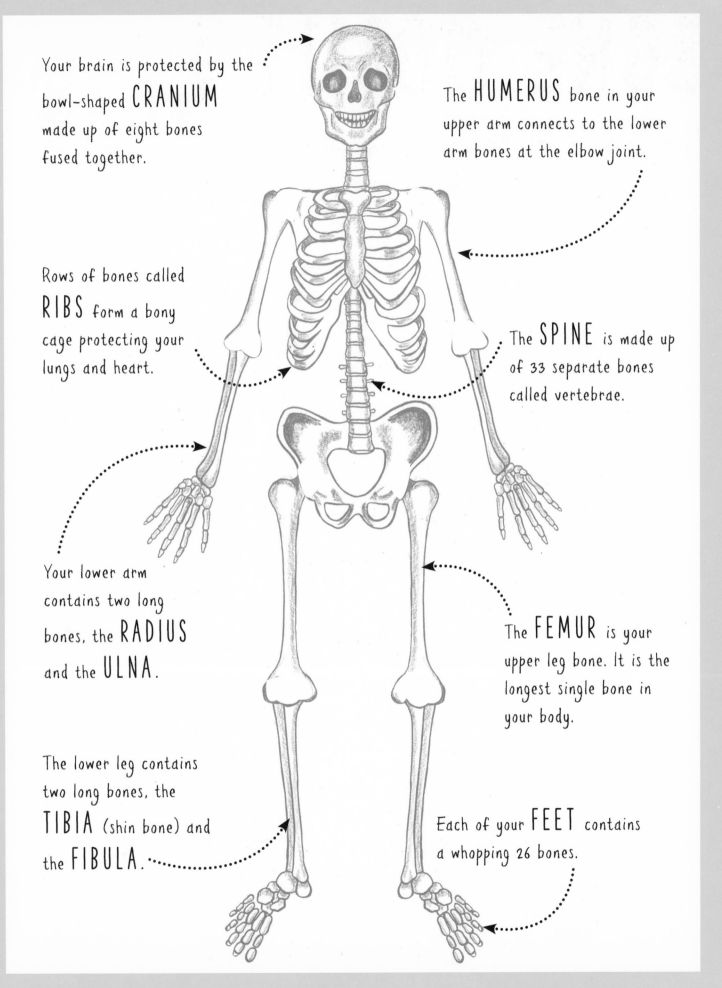

Your brain is protected by the bowl-shaped CRANIUM made up of eight bones fused together.

The HUMERUS bone in your upper arm connects to the lower arm bones at the elbow joint.

Rows of bones called RIBS form a bony cage protecting your lungs and heart.

The SPINE is made up of 33 separate bones called vertebrae.

Your lower arm contains two long bones, the RADIUS and the ULNA.

The FEMUR is your upper leg bone. It is the longest single bone in your body.

The lower leg contains two long bones, the TIBIA (shin bone) and the FIBULA.

Each of your FEET contains a whopping 26 bones.

BONE MOBILE

Trace or copy these templates onto white cardboard.

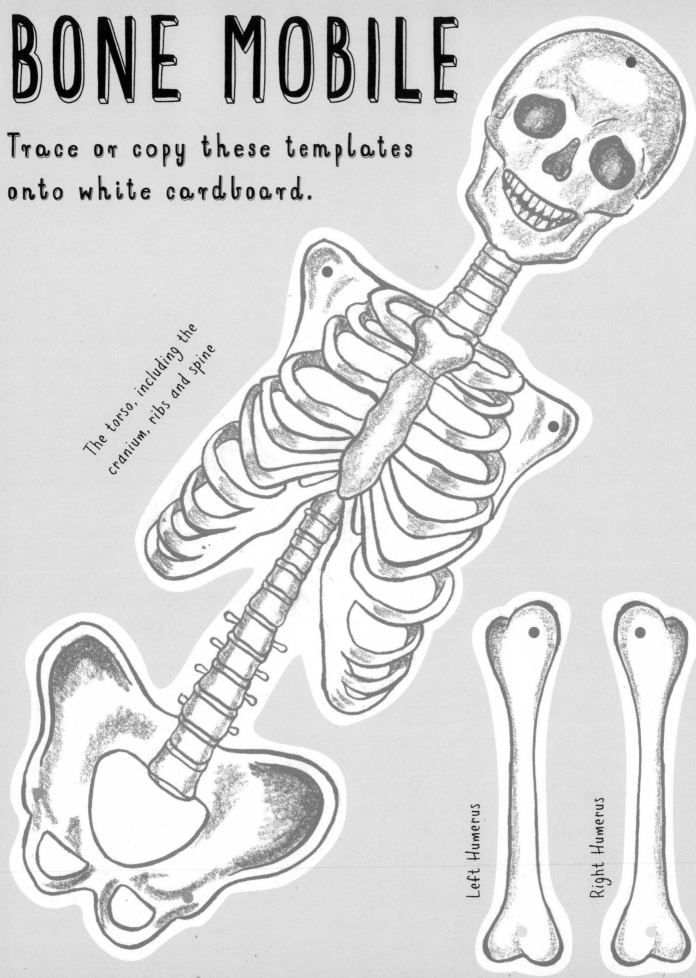

The torso, including the cranium, ribs and spine

Left Humerus

Right Humerus

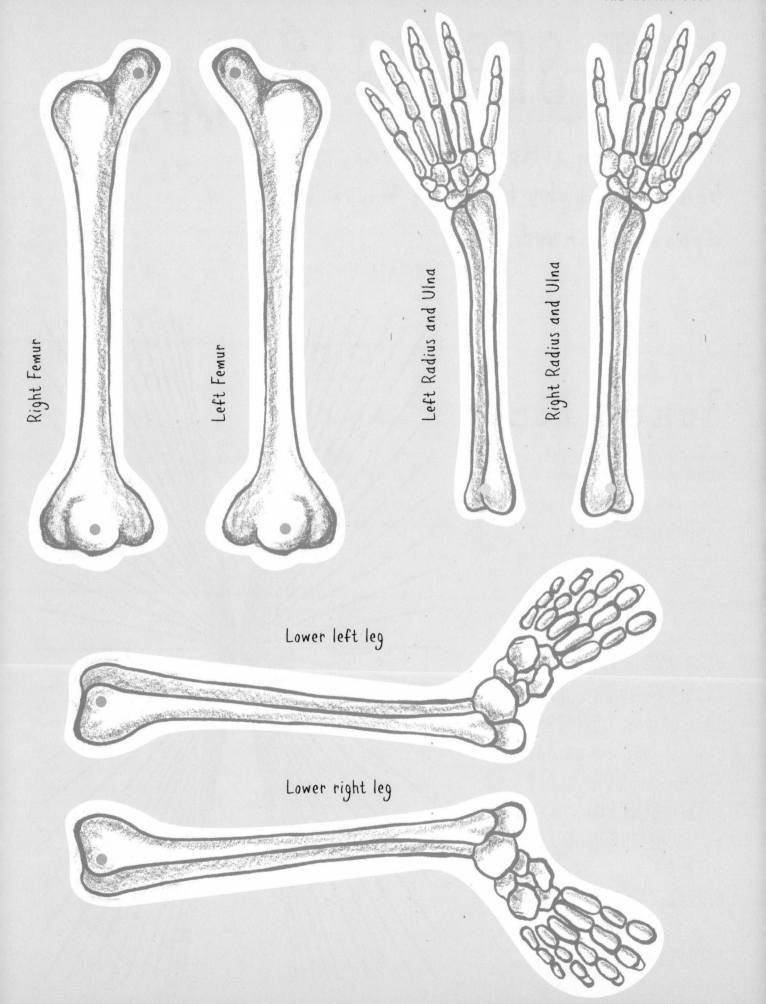

Right Femur

Left Femur

Left Radius and Ulna

Right Radius and Ulna

Lower left leg

Lower right leg

NOT SEEING STRAIGHT

With these simple illusions, you can bend straight lines or make them appear slanted.

Start your lines here.

Bendy Lines

Using a ruler and a thick red pen, draw two long, straight vertical lines connecting the red dots.

YOUR TWO STRAIGHT LINES SUDDENLY DON'T LOOK QUITE SO STRAIGHT, DO THEY? YOU'VE JUST DRAWN THE HERING ILLUSION, NAMED AFTER THE GERMAN SCIENTIST EWALD HERING, WHO CAME UP WITH THE IDEA. THE LINES APPEAR TO BULGE BECAUSE OF HOW YOUR BRAIN VIEWS THE RADIATING LINES.

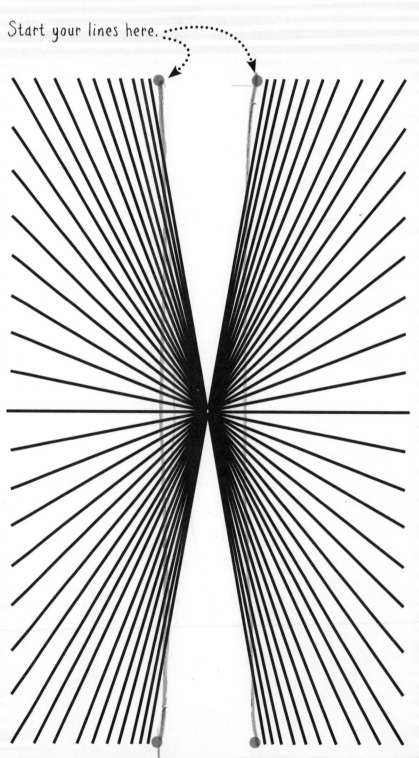

Get in Line

THIS ILLUSION WAS FIRST DISCOVERED WHEN A
SCIENTIST WENT FOR A CUP OF TEA IN A CAFE AND
DISCOVERED THE TILE PATTERN ON THE CAFE'S WALLS!

Using a blue pen, color every
other tile on this page.

THE WAY THE TILES ARE STAGGERED CAUSES THE BRAIN TO THINK THAT EACH
ROW OF TILES DIPS OR RISE, BUT IF YOU RUN A RULER OVER THEM, YOU'LL SEE
THAT THEY ARE ALL PERFECTLY PARALLEL... **EYE-MAZING!**

LEAF BRIEF

HAVE YOU EVER LOOKED AT THE DIFFERENT SHAPES OF LEAVES? SOME ARE SIMPLE, WITH A SINGLE LEAF BLADE. OTHERS, CALLED COMPOUND LEAVES, ARE MADE UP OF A NUMBER OF BLADES KNOWN AS LEAFLETS.

VEINS transport nutrients and water.

SIMPLE LEAF

The main flat part of a leaf is called the BLADE.

BUDS are future leaves, tightly folded up.

Leaves are where a plant's food is made from sunlight, water and carbon dioxide. Scientists call this process PHOTOSYNTHESIS.

COMPOUND LEAF

The stalk is also called the PETIOLE.

Some leaf blades are divided into LOBES.

LEAF RUBBINGS

You can investigate the different types of leaves by making rubbings of them.

1 Choose a leaf with an interesting shape. Place it vein side up onto a piece of cardboard, a small craft mat or a strong piece of fiberboard.

2 Place the board, with the leaf, underneath this page. Rub over the page with a crayon. The leaf and its features will magically appear!

IN A SPIN

Learn the science behind spinning with this cool ROTOCOPTOR.

1 Trace the template onto thin cardboard or use the template at the back of this book and stick onto cardboard.

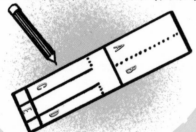

2 Cut carefully along the three dotted lines. Bend tab A away from you and bend tab B toward you so that both tabs are at an angle to the ground. Bend tabs C and D inward so they fold over each other.

3 Fold up tab E and clip it in place using a metal paper clip.

4 Now, watch your new creation fly! Grip it at the bottom, throw it high into the air and watch the two blades make it spin around as it slowly descends to the ground.

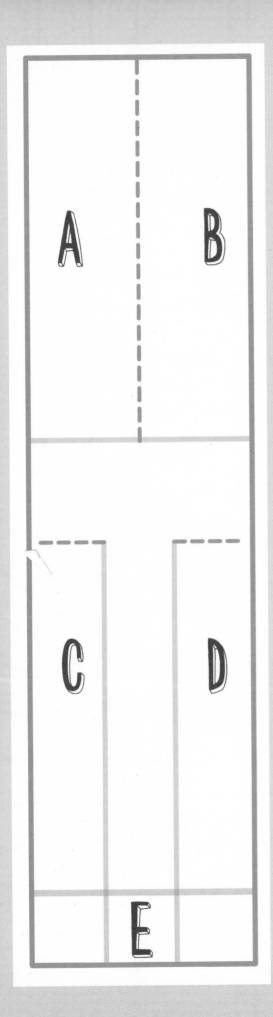

Color both sides of your rotocopter with any design you like.

ONCE YOUR ROTOCOPTER IS UP AND FLYING, TRY PLACING ONE OR MORE CUPS AND BOWLS ON THE GROUND, THEN STAND ON A CHAIR AND SEE IF YOU CAN GET YOUR ROTOCOPTER TO SPIN DOWN ONTO YOUR TARGETS. OR GET YOUR FRIENDS TO MAKE THEIR OWN ROTOCOPTERS, THEN TIME WHOSE CAN STAY IN THE AIR THE LONGEST.

Spin Science

How does a rotocopter work? When it starts falling toward the ground, air pushes up against the two blades. It is because the blades are angled that some of the pushing force of the air, known as thrust, pushes sideways. This sideways thrust forces each blade to turn on either side of the rotocopter, causing the whole craft to spin.

IN PERSPECTIVE

YOUR BRAIN EXPECTS OBJECTS FARTHER AWAY TO LOOK SMALLER. THIS ALLOWS YOU TO CREATE FUN PERSPECTIVE ILLUSIONS.

TAKE A LOOK AT THESE TWO PEOPLE. IS ONE PERSON LARGER THAN THE OTHER?

In fact, they are exactly the same size! What's happening? The narrowing lines trick our brain into thinking that the person on the right is farther in the distance. So, your brain figures that to appear at that size in the distance, the "farther away" person must be larger than the "closer" one.

Now create your own perspective illusion! Draw any two identical objects you like along this corridor, one at the back and one at the front. Trace the object to make sure both drawings are exactly the same size.

Does one look bigger than the other?

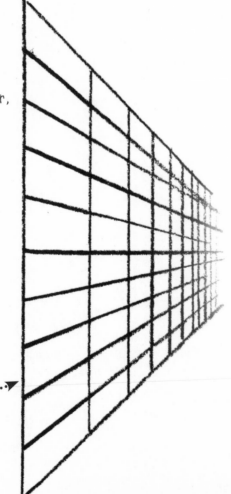

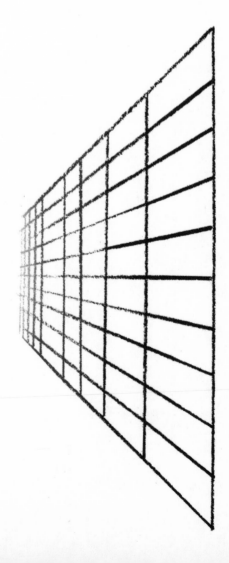

AMES ROOM

THIS GREAT ILLUSION IS NAMED AFTER AN AMERICAN OPTICIAN, ADELBERT AMES, JR. HE INVENTED THIS CRAZY ROOM THAT USES DISTORTED PERSPECTIVE TO TRICK THE BRAIN INTO SEEING THINGS INSIDE THE ROOM AS BEING OF DIFFERENT SIZES THAN THEY REALLY ARE.

1 Trace the two templates on the next two pages onto stiff white cardboard. If you prefer, you can cut out the templates at the back of this book and stick them onto white cardboard.

2 Now decorate your room! Draw pictures inside the picture frames. If tracing, color the alternating floor tiles to match the template.

3 Cut out the two pieces of the room. You will also need to cut out the peephole and the section of the roof marked by a red line.

4 Bend all of the tabs inward along the dotted lines. Use tape to join the tabs that hold all the walls together. Your room is complete!

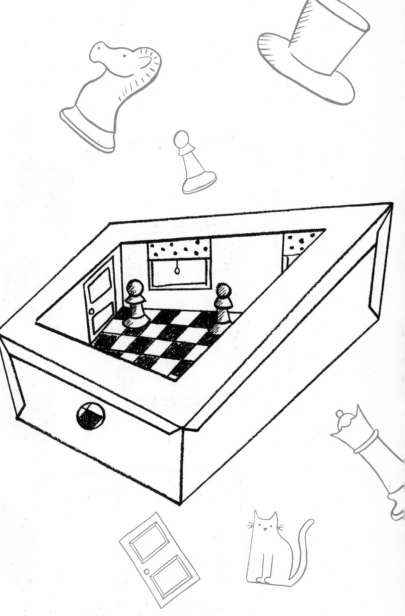

NOW PLACE TWO SAME-SIZED OBJECTS (SUCH AS SMALL FIGURES OR CHESS PIECES) IN THE ROOM, ONE AT EACH OF THE FAR CORNERS. PEER THROUGH THE PEEPHOLE. IT LOOKS LIKE TWO FIGURES ARE STANDING IN THE BACK CORNERS OF A PERFECTLY SQUARE ROOM, AND ONE FIGURE IS A LOT BIGGER THAN THE OTHER. SWAP THE FIGURES OVER AND LOOK AGAIN— ONE FIGURE HAS SHRUNK AND ONE HAS GROWN!

Trace these templates onto stiff white cardboard, then cut out and color.

Color the walls all the same color.

Color every other floor tile to match this pattern.

Draw your own pictures inside the frames.

Add in the view outside the window.

Remember to cut out these parts before you tape the room together!

FLIP SDOTHS

SOME PICTURES HAVE MORE THAN ONE MEANING. THESE ARE CALLED AMBIGUOUS IMAGES.

Ambiguous images can cause your brain to flip back and forth between two explanations of the same picture. Sometimes your brain simply cannot decide which explanation is the most likely. On the right, is a drawing of a rabbit ...

A   B   C

4 3 2 1

1   2   3   4

A B C

... Copy the rabbit here, but rotate it clockwise by 90 degrees. What do you see now? Color the new creature!

Using a ruler, connect the dots to form a simple, six-sided figure that looks like a greeting card.

Now take another look. Are you looking at the INSIDE of the card or the OUTSIDE? There is no correct answer.

Now design and color either the inside or outside of your card. It's up to you!

DRAW THE IMPOSSIBLE

IMPOSSIBLE IMAGES ARE PICTURES THAT BAMBOOZLE YOUR BRAIN. THEY CAUSE
A CONFLICT BETWEEN WHAT YOUR EYES SEE AND WHAT YOUR BRAIN MAKES OF THEM.

Baffling Blivets

Using a black pen, draw a vertical
line to join the two dots marked "A."
Then do the same for the two dots
marked "B."

YOU HAVE COMPLETED AN IMPOSSIBLE
IMAGE CALLED A BLIVET OR DEVIL'S
PITCHFORK. DOES IT HAVE TWO OR
THREE PRONGS STICKING OUT?
IT'S HARD FOR YOUR BRAIN TO TELL.

THIS ILLUSION
WORKS BECAUSE YOUR
BRAIN SEEKS OUT FAMILIAR
OBJECTS AND OFTEN TURNS
2-D DRAWINGS INTO
3-D OBJECTS.

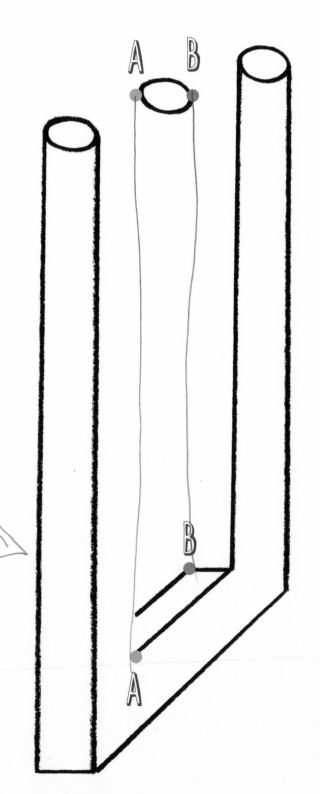
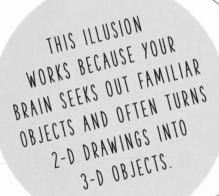

Crazy Square

1 Join the four dots below to form a square.

2 Add ½-inch-long lines to each of the corners.

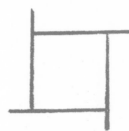

3 Draw four more lines starting at the corner lines, as shown. Make sure they extend a little bit beyond the corners.

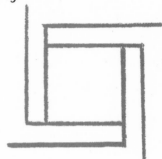

4 Add a 45-degree angle to the end of each line.

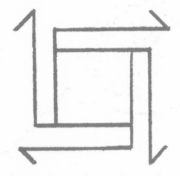

5 Connect all the lines as shown.

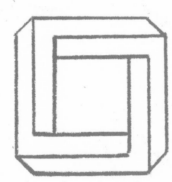

Congratulations! You have drawn an impossible square.

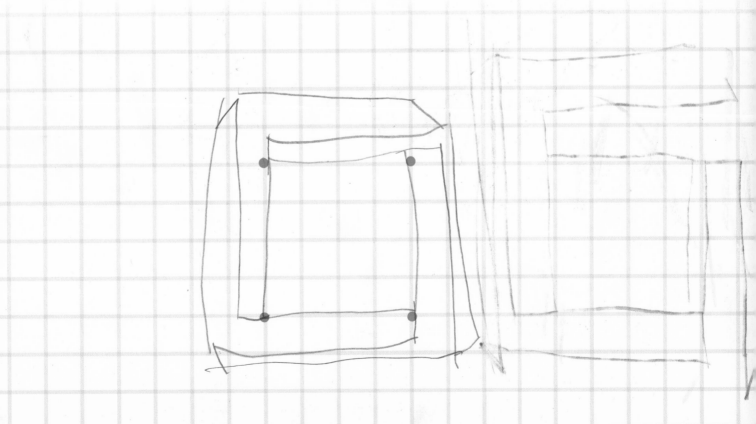

BUTTERFLY LIFE CYCLE

BEFORE THEY BECOME BEAUTIFUL BUTTERFLIES, THESE INSECTS GO THROUGH INCREDIBLE CHANGES IN HOW THEY LOOK. USE YOUR PENS OR PENCILS TO COLOR THEIR LIFE CYCLE.

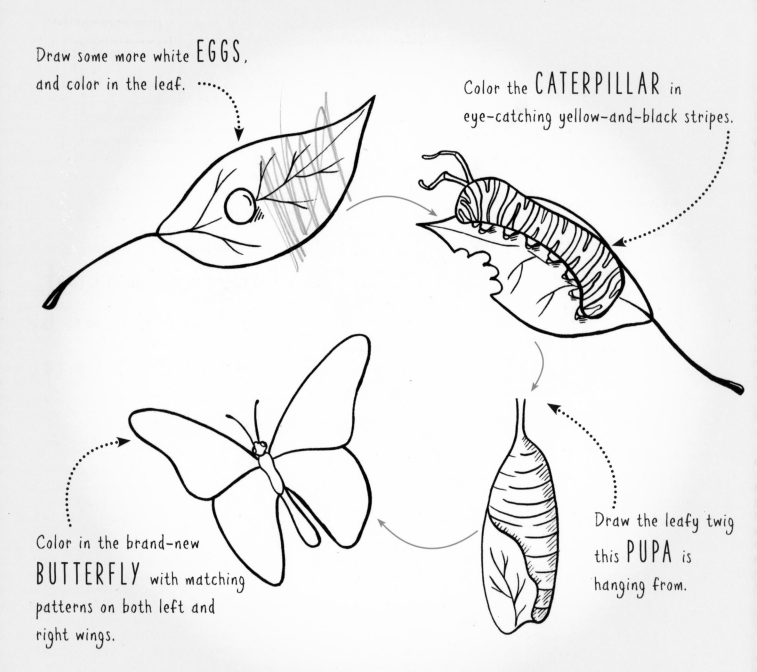

Draw some more white EGGS, and color in the leaf.

Color the CATERPILLAR in eye-catching yellow-and-black stripes.

Color in the brand-new BUTTERFLY with matching patterns on both left and right wings.

Draw the leafy twig this PUPA is hanging from.

Eggs are often laid on leaves or plant stems. Out hatch caterpillars, which shed their skin four or five times as they eat lots and grow rapidly. The caterpillar turns into an adult butterfly inside a case called a chrysalis or pupa. The butterfly emerges from the pupa with soft, wet wings that quickly dry and harden.

Colorful Creatures

BUTTERFLIES FLY USING TWO PAIRS OF WINGS, WHICH ARE OFTEN BRIGHTLY PATTERNED. COLOR THE WINGS OF THIS BEAUTIFUL PEACOCK BUTTERFLY, WHICH LIVES IN EUROPE AND ASIA.

ANTENNA

These long feelers help butterflies to smell and to keep their balance when flying.

PROBOSCIS

This tube unrolls so that butterflies can sip their liquid food, often nectar from flowers.

HEAD

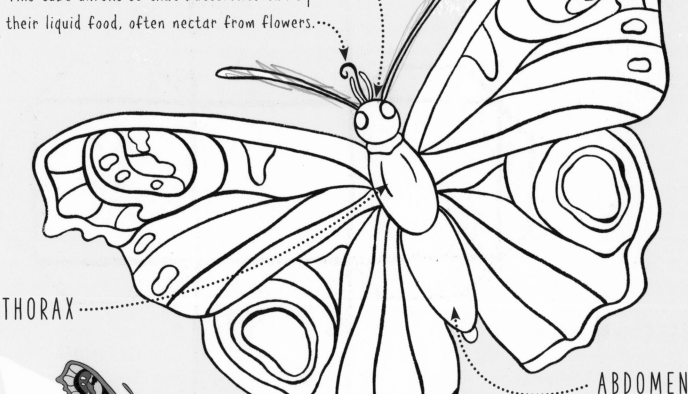

THORAX

ABDOMEN

WINGS

A butterfly's wings are covered in scales over a frame of veins.

LEGS

A butterfly can smell and taste using special cells on their six legs.

BRAIN STRAINERS

YOUR CLEVER BRAIN ALLOWS YOU TO THINK, LEARN AND SOLVE PROBLEMS. DID YOU KNOW THAT THERE ARE MANY DIFFERENT WAYS YOU CAN BE INTELLIGENT? YOU MIGHT BE SUPER SMART AT MATH OR MUSIC, FOR EXAMPLE, OR VERY BRIGHT AT UNDERSTANDING OTHER PEOPLE. THE CHALLENGES ON THE NEXT FEW PAGES TEST SOME OF THE DIFFERENT WAYS YOU CAN BE BRAINY.

The first two puzzles test your
SPATIAL INTELLIGENCE— how
good you are at working with shapes,
spaces and pictures.

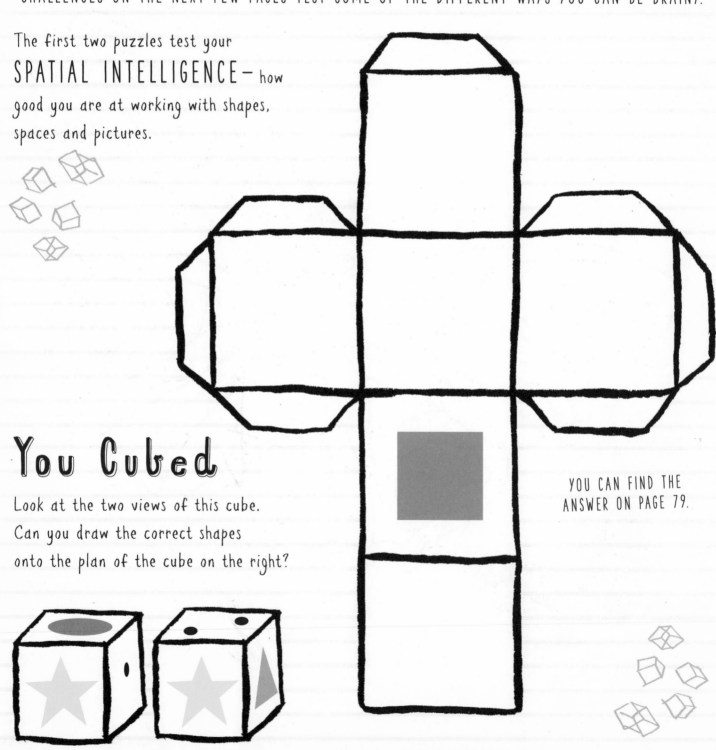

You Cubed

Look at the two views of this cube.
Can you draw the correct shapes
onto the plan of the cube on the right?

YOU CAN FIND THE
ANSWER ON PAGE 79.

Tennis Triangle

By moving three of these tennis balls, can you make the triangle point down instead of up?

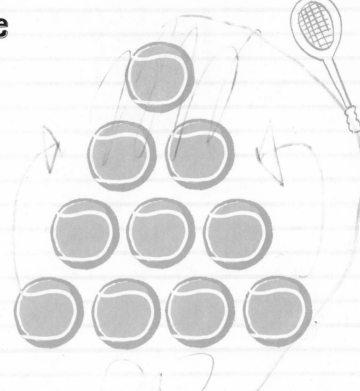

In the Envelope

This tough visual test challenges your LATERAL THINKING—that's thinking in creative and unusual ways to solve a problem.

1 First, without taking your pen or pencil off the page, can you draw this envelope without going back over a line already drawn?

2 Too easy? Now let's make it harder! Can you do the same but this time WITHOUT crossing another line while you are drawing?

YOU CAN FIND THE ANSWERS ON PAGE 80.

FIGURE IT OUT

THE PREVIOUS PAGE TESTED YOUR SPATIAL INTELLIGENCE AND LATERAL
THINKING. NOW IT'S TIME TO TEST YOUR LOGIC SKILLS.

Shape Sudoku

Fill in this Sudoku puzzle using the six colored
shapes. Make sure you follow the rules below.

Each ROW should contain all six shapes.

Each COLUMN should contain all six shapes.

Each of these
six mini-grids
should contain
all six shapes.

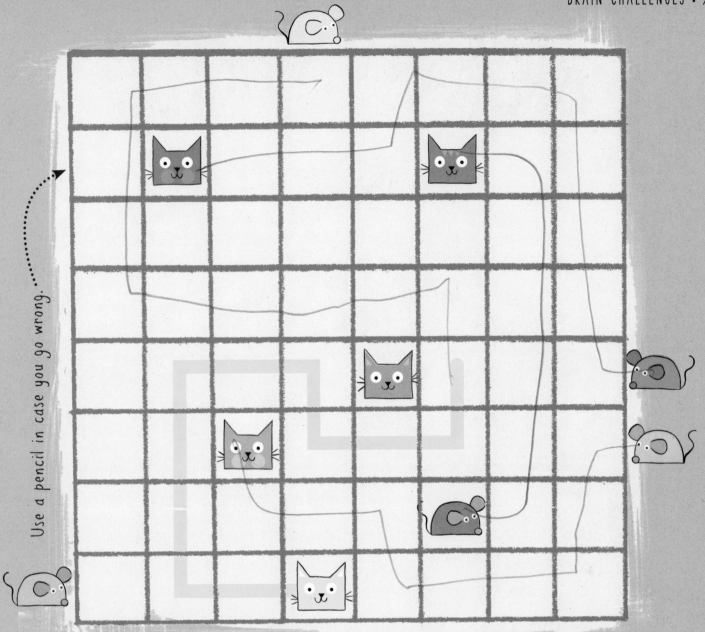

Use a pencil in case you go wrong.

Cat and Mouse

Can you guide each of these cats to the toy mouse of the matching color? The cats can move horizontally (left and right) and vertically (up and down), but not diagonally, and no paths must cross.

YOU CAN FIND THE ANSWERS ON PAGE 80.

MEMORY CIRCUS

YOUR BRAIN HAS DIFFERENT AREAS FOR SHORT-TERM AND LONG-TERM MEMORIES.

SHORT-TERM MEMORY CAN HOLD A FEW ITEMS FOR 20–30 SECONDS BEFORE THEY ARE FORGOTTEN.

★ TEST YOUR SHORT-TERM MEMORY WITH THIS SIMPLE CHALLENGE. ★

Stare at this list of objects found at a circus for 30 seconds. Then cover the page with a piece of paper, and draw all the objects you can remember on the blank page opposite. Don't peek!

Chair

Balloon

Circus performer

Ladder

Ice-cream cone

Drum

Clown

Bicycle

Top hat

Juggling pins

Bucket of water

Custard pie

If your brain focuses on an item in its short-term memory, there's a chance it will pass into long-term memory. This is your brain's main store of memories. Facts, experiences and how you perform different skills are all held in long-term memory.

CAN YOU RECALL THEM ALL?

HOW MANY OBJECTS DID
YOU REMEMBER?

0-4 = could do better

5-9 = good

10-12 = outstanding!

TAKE IT FURTHER

Not sure what to do next? Here are some ideas for creative science projects.

IDEAS FOR PROJECTS

Use a mirror to take a look at your own eyes (pages 24-25) and then draw one of them. What color are your irises? Color them to match. Notice how big or small your pupil is, and draw it the same size. What does the size of your pupil tell you about how much light there is in the room?

Make several rubbings of different leaves using different colors (page 55) on separate pieces of paper. Cut them out and glue them down to make a colorful collage.

Think up your own memory test like the one on pages 72-73 to test your friends and family. It should contain between 12 and 20 different objects.

Use a mirror to help you write a coded message, using mirror image letters. Remember, in a mirror image, left and right are reversed (page 39).

Can you draw other types of flowers and label them like you did on page 13?

Use colored glue to paint the outline of the apple (page 26) onto a piece of clear plastic. Use colored paints to color the apple light blue with a pink leaf to make an afterimage stained glass pendant!

Can you draw an impossible triangle, using the same technique that was shown for drawing an impossible square on page 65? Give it a try!

Afterimages (pages 26-27) work with black and white as well as colors. Try designing your own simple black-and-white image. Stare at your completed image for 45 seconds, then look at a blank piece of white paper. You should see the black and white reversed.

PUT IT TOGETHER

Make some more leaf prints (page 55), but this time by bashing them! Hapa Zome is the Japanese art of pounding leaves and flowers to extract the dye from them. Place a moist leaf or flower inside a folded piece of cotton fabric on a hard surface, and gently pound with a mallet or stone.

Now that you've learned about rainbows (page 36), why not make your own? Place a glass of water in bright, direct sunlight. The white light from the Sun should separate into different colors as it passes through the water. Line up a piece of paper with the rainbow and then color it in.

Once you've completed the memory test on pages 72-73, here's an extra challenge to test your visual memory. Stare at your drawings for 30 seconds, then look away and write down all the objects you remember.

Make a mini-movie (page 32) showing the cycle of the Moon (page 44).

Copy some of the optical illusions in the book onto small pieces of cardboard. Draw a frame around the edge of each piece, and use a loop of tape to decorate the walls of your Ames Room (pages 59-61).

Make an X-ray thaumatrope (page 30) by drawing a person on one side and their skeleton (page 49) on the other.

Make your own optical illusions bookmark by copying two of your favorite illusions from this book onto either side of a strip of thick cardboard.

GLOSSARY

ABSORB: to soak up something; for example, dark colors absorb lots of light.

ALTERNATING: a word meaning every other one. So, the alternating letters of the word "GLOVE" would be G, O and E.

ANGLE: the space measured in degrees between lines that meet in a single point.

ARACHNIDS: a class of creatures that are wingless, have eight legs and a two-part body. Spiders and scorpions are arachnids.

CARBON DIOXIDE: a colorless gas without any smell, found in the air. It is created by people and many other creatures when they breathe and release energy from their bodies, as well as by burning things.

CELLS: tiny units that form the building blocks of all living things. Some simple, tiny creatures are made up of just one cell, while complex creatures, like people, are made up of millions of different types of cells.

CLOCKWISE: to travel in a circular direction in the same way as the hands of a clock move around a clock face.

COMPASS: a drawing tool used for making perfect circles.

CRANIUM: the bowl-shaped collection of bones that surround and protect your brain.

DIAMETER: the distance across a circle in a straight line passing through the circle's center.

DISTORTION: the changing of a thing from its normal shape.

DYES: substances that change the color of something such as fabric or paper.

ENERGY: the ability to do work. There are many different types of energy, from the chemical energy in food, to heat, light and electricity. Sometimes energy is converted from one type to another, such as when electrical energy is turned into heat energy in a teakettle.

EXPLANATIONS: thoughts, demonstrations or statements that make something clear or easy to understand.

FERTILIZATION: in plants, the process that makes a plant able to produce seeds.

FOCUS: adjustments made to your eyes so that you can see something clearly and concentrate on it.

GRAVITY: a force that tries to pull two objects toward each other. When one object is much more massive than another, it will pull objects toward it, which is why objects fall down toward Earth's surface.

GRID: a background of squares on paper or material made by crossing horizontal and vertical lines.

HAND-EYE COORDINATION: the ability to perform tasks that require your hands and eyes to work together, such as drawing a picture or catching a ball.

HORIZONTAL: a word that describes a line that extends from side to side.

IDENTICAL: exactly the same as something else.

INFLUENCE: the power to alter or affect someone or something.

INSECT: a small creature with no spine, six legs, a three-part body, and usually, pairs of wings.

JOINTS: the place or parts where two bones in a skeleton meet. Some joints, such as the elbow and knee, allow movement.

LIFE CYCLE: the series of changes that a living thing goes through from birth to death.

MEMORY: the ability to remember things. Also a term used to describe parts of your brain used to store experiences, thoughts and how to perform skills.

OPTICAL ILLUSION: a picture or object that tricks your eyes and brain into thinking the picture or object is something that it is not.

PERISCOPE: a tubelike device containing mirrors that allow people to view things, usually above them, that are out of sight otherwise.

PERSISTENCE OF VISION: term used to describe how the eye keeps hold of things that it sees for a fraction of a second after viewing them.

PERSPECTIVE: the way of drawing 3-D scenes or objects on a 2-D (flat) surface so that they appear to have height, width and depth.

PETALS: the colored outer parts of a flower that protect the delicate parts inside and, in some cases, attract insects and other creatures.

POLLEN: fine powdery grains, often yellow colored, found inside a plant's flowers, which help plants make seeds.

RECTANGULAR: an object that has the shape of a rectangle—a shape with four straight sides joined by right angles at the corners with opposite sides of equal lengths.

REFLECTED: to bounce or throw back something such as light, heat or sound, without absorbing it.

SKULL: the part of the skeleton made up of bones that form the protective framework of your head.

STAR: a giant, hot ball of gas. The nearest star is the Sun. All other stars you can see as small dots of white light in the night sky.

THAUMATROPE: a classic toy made up of a disk with different drawings on either side. When spun fast, the two drawings merge into one image.

UNIVERSE: all of space and everything in it, including the Sun, stars, and our own planet, Earth.

VERTICAL: a word that describes a line that extends up and down.

WINGSPAN: the distance across a bird or insect's wings measured from wingtip to wingtip.

ANSWERS

!! The illusions on this page work best when seen from a distance.

Page 22: Color Confusion

Page 34: Shifting Circle

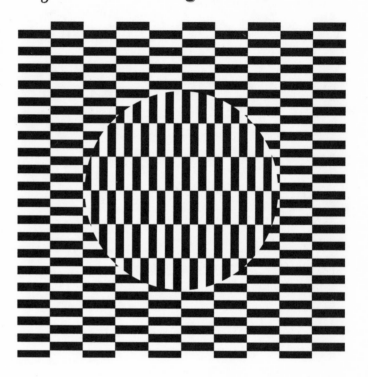

Page 23: Red Squares

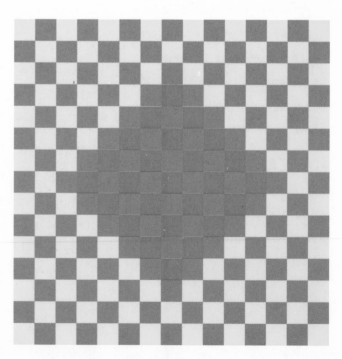

Page 35: Spinning Rings

Page 68: You Cubed

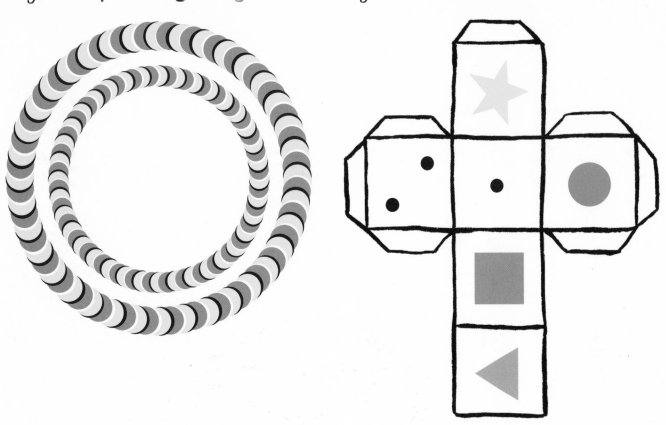

Page 41: Bouncing Around

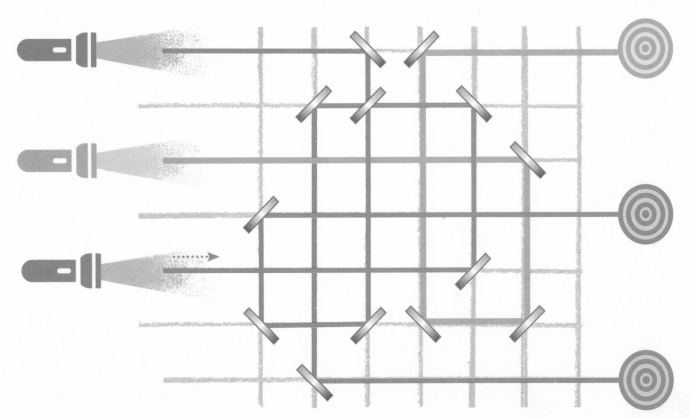

Page 69: Tennis Triangle

Page 69: In the Envelope

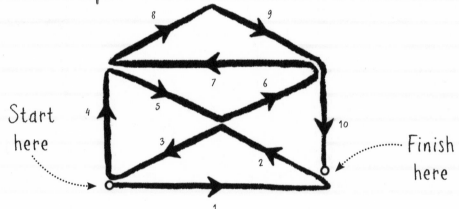

Page 70: Shape Sudoku

Page 71: Cat and Mouse